New Light

Bible Stories

NEW INTERNATIONAL READER'S VERSION

Hodder & Stoughton
LONDON SYDNEY AUCKLAND

New Light Bible Stories
New International Reader's Version
© 1999 John Hunt Publishing, Alresford, Hants, UK

First published in Great Britain in 1999
by Hodder & Stoughton Ltd
338 Euston Road,
London NW1 3BH

10 9 8 7 6 5 4 3 2 1

ISBN 0 340 65177 6

Scripture quotations taken from the Holy Bible,
New International Reader's Version,
Copyright © 1996, 1998 by International Bible Society.
Edited by Jean Watson, with permission.

Illustrations copyright © 1999 Susan Wintringham
The right of Susan Wintringham to be identified as the illustrator of the
work has been asserted by her in accordance with the Copyright,
Designs and Patents Act 1988.

All rights reserved. No part of this publication may be reproduced,
stored in a retrieval system, or transmitted, in any form or by any
means without the prior written permission of the publisher, nor be
otherwise circulated in any form of binding or cover than that in
which it is published and without a similar condition being
imposed on the subsequent purchaser.

Designed by The Bridgewater Book Company Ltd, Lewes
Printed and bound in Singapore by Tien Wah Press (PTE) Ltd

This book belongs to

....

Contents

Old Testament stories

In the beginning 5

The Garden of Eden 9

Noah and the ark 14

Joseph's beautiful robe 19

Pharaoh's dreams 25

Joseph and his brothers 30

Moses and the burning bush 37

The plagues of Egypt 40

The great escape 47

David and Goliath 49

Daniel in the lions' den 53

Jonah and the storm 58

New Testament Stories

Angels and shepherds 62

Three wise men 65

Loaves and fishes 68

Walking on water 72

The good Samaritan 75

The loving Father 79

Zacchaeus the tax collector 85

The road to Easter 87

Good Friday 91

The empty tomb 94

In the beginning

In the beginning, God created the heavens and the earth.
At that time, the ocean covered the earth.

The Spirit of God was hovering over the waters.

God said, "Let there be light." And there was light.
He separated the light from the darkness.
God called the light "day".
He called the darkness "night".

It was day one.

God said, "Let there be a great space between the waters."
God called the great space "sky".

It was day two.

God said, "Let the water under the sky be gathered into one place. Let dry ground appear." God called the dry ground "land". He called the waters that were gathered together "oceans".

Then God said, "Let the land produce plants. Let each kind of plant or tree have its own kind of seed."

The land produced plants. Each kind of plant had its own kind of seed.

It was day three.

God said, "Let there be lights in the great space of the sky." God made two lights.
He made the larger light to rule over the day. He made the smaller light to rule over the night.

It was day four.

God said, "Let the waters be filled with living things.
Let birds fly above the earth." He created every living and moving thing that fills the waters. He created every kind of bird that flies.

God blessed them. He said, "Have little ones and grow in number."

It was day five.

God said, "Let the land produce all kinds of living creatures."
He made all kinds of creatures that move along the ground.

Then God said, "Let us make man in our likeness." So God created man in his own likeness.

Then God said, "I am giving you every tree that has fruit with seed in it. I am giving every green plant to all the land animals and the birds of the air for food."

God saw everything he had made. And it was very good.

It was day six.

By the seventh day God had finished the work he had been doing. So on the seventh day he rested from all his work. God blessed the seventh day and made it holy.

The Garden of Eden

The Lord God planted a garden in the east. It was Eden.

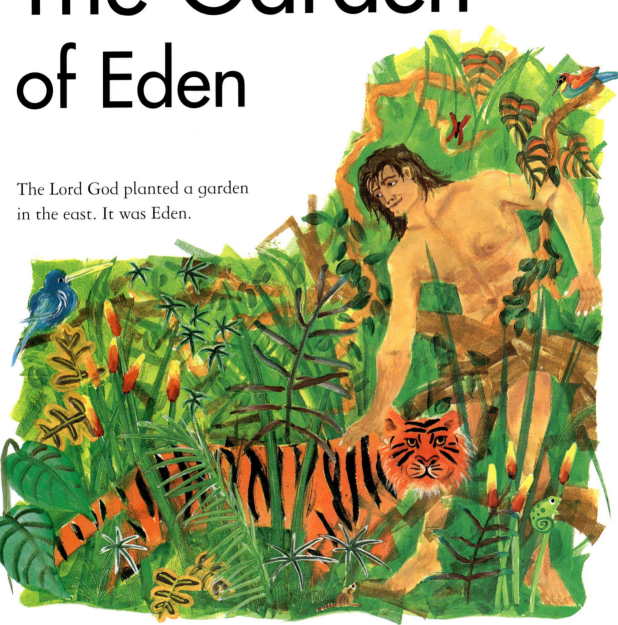

There he put the man he had formed. He put him there to work its ground and to look after it.

He said, "You can eat the fruit of any tree that is in the garden. But you must not eat the fruit of the tree of the knowledge of good and evil. If you do, you can be sure that you will die."

The Lord God said, "It is not good for the man to be alone. I will make a helper who is just right for him."

The man gave names to all the animals. But Adam didn't find a helper that was right for him.

Then the Lord God made a woman. He made her from the rib he had taken out of the man. And he brought her to him.

The man said, "She will be named 'woman' because she was taken out of a man." That's why a man will leave his father and mother and be joined to his wife. The two of them will become one.

The serpent was more clever than any of the wild animals the Lord God had made.

The serpent said to the woman, "Did God really say, 'You must not eat of the fruit of any tree in the garden'?"

The woman said, "God said, 'You must not eat the fruit of the tree in the middle of the garden. If you do, you will die.'"

"You can be sure that you won't die," the serpent said. "You will be able to tell the difference between good and evil. You will be like God."

The woman took some of the fruit and ate it. She also gave some to her husband and he ate it.

Then they hid from the Lord God among the trees of the garden.

But the Lord God called out to the man, "Have you eaten the fruit of the tree I commanded you not to eat?"

The man said, "The woman gave me some fruit from the tree and I ate it."

Then the Lord God said to the woman, "What have you done?"

The woman said, "The serpent tricked me."

The Garden of Eden

The Lord God spoke to the serpent. He said, "I am putting a curse on you. You will eat dust all the days of your life."

The Lord God said to the woman, "You will be in pain when you have children. You will long for your husband. And he will rule over you."

The Lord God said to Adam, "I am putting a curse on the ground because of what you did. All the days of your life you will have to work hard to get food from the ground."

Then the Lord God drove the man out of the Garden of Eden.

Noah and the ark

Men began to grow in number on the earth,
and daughters were born to them.

The Lord saw how bad the sins of man had become on the earth.
All the thoughts in his heart were always turned only towards
what was evil.

The Lord was very sad that he had made man on the earth.
His heart was filled with pain.

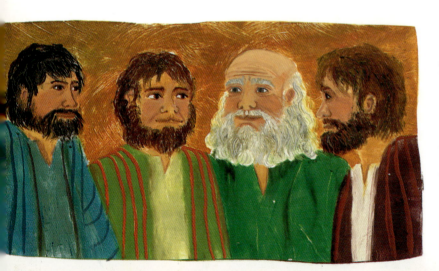

But the Lord was
pleased with Noah.
Noah was a good man.
He walked with God.

Noah had three sons.
Their names were Shem,
Ham and Japheth.

NOAH AND THE ARK

God said to Noah, "Make yourself an ark out of cypress wood. I am going to bring a flood on the earth. But I will make my covenant with you."

Noah did everything exactly as God commanded him.

Then the Lord said to Noah, "Go into the ark with your whole family."

Noah and his sons entered the ark. His wife and his sons' wives went with them. Pairs of all living creatures that breathe came to Noah and entered the ark. The animals going in were male and female of every living thing.

NEW LIGHT BIBLE STORIES

For 40 days the flood kept coming on the earth. As the waters rose higher, they lifted the ark high above the earth.

The ark floated on the water. The waters continued to rise until they covered the mountains.

Every living thing that moved on the earth died. Only Noah and those who were with him in the ark were left.

God sent a wind over the earth. At the end of 150 days the water had gone down. The ark came to rest on the mountains of Ararat.

Noah opened the window he had made in the ark. He sent a raven out. It kept flying back and forth until the water had dried up from the earth.

Then God said to Noah, "Come out of the ark."

So Noah came out of the ark. His sons and his wife and his sons' wives were with him. All the animals came out of the ark.

Then Noah built an altar to honour the Lord. He sacrificed burnt offerings to the Lord on the altar.

Then God gave his blessing to Noah and his sons. He said to them, "Have children and grow in number. Fill the earth. Every living thing is put under your control.

"Here is my covenant that I am making with you. A flood will never destroy the earth again.

"Here is the sign of the covenant I am making. I have put my rainbow in the clouds. When the rainbow appears in the clouds, I will see it. I will remember that my covenant will last for ever. It is a covenant between me and every kind of living thing on earth."

Joseph's beautiful robe

People grew in number on the earth.
Jacob and his family lived in the land of Canaan.

Now Jacob loved Joseph more than his other sons.
He made him a beautiful robe.

Joseph's brothers saw that their father
loved him more than any of them.
So they hated Joseph.

Joseph had a dream.
When he told it to his brothers,
they hated him even more.

He said, "We were tying up sheaves of corn out in the field.
Your sheaves gathered round my sheaf and bowed down to it."

His brothers said, 'Do you plan to be king over us?'

Joseph had another dream. He told his father as well as his brothers, "This time the sun and moon and 11 stars were bowing down to me."

His father told him off. He said, "Will your mother and I and your 11 brothers really bow down to the ground in front of you?"

His brothers were jealous of him. But his father kept the matter in mind.

Joseph's Beautiful Robe

Joseph's brothers had gone to look after their father's flocks. Jacob said to Joseph, "Go to your brothers. See how they are doing. Then come back and tell me."

Joseph went to look for his brothers. They saw him a long way off. Before he reached them, they made plans to kill him.

"Here comes that dreamer!" they said. "Let's kill him. Let's say that a wild animal ate him up. Then we'll see whether his dreams will come true."

NEW LIGHT BIBLE STORIES

But one brother, Reuben, tried to save
Joseph. "Let's not take his life,"
he said. "Throw him into this
empty well here in the desert."

When Joseph came to his brothers,
he was wearing his beautiful robe.
They took it away from him.
And they threw him into the well.

Then they sat down
to eat their meal.

Joseph's Beautiful Robe

Some traders were coming past. Their camels were loaded
with spices and myrrh.

Judah said, "What will we gain if we kill our brother?
Let's sell him to these traders. Let's not harm him ourselves.
After all, he's our brother."

Joseph's brothers pulled him out of the well.
They sold him to the traders. Then the traders took him to Egypt.

The brothers got Joseph's robe.
They killed a goat and dipped the robe in the blood.

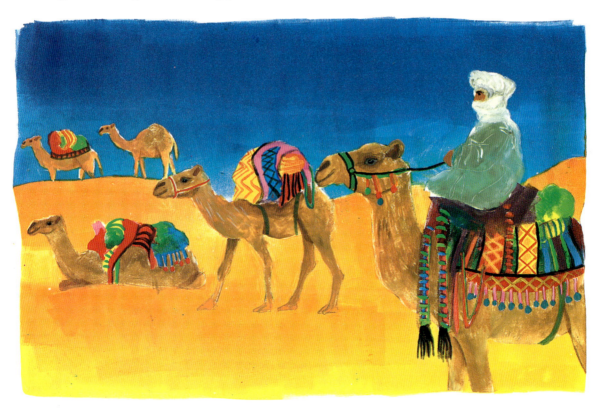

They took the beautiful robe back to their father.
They said, "We found this."

Jacob recognised it. He said, "It is my son's robe!
A wild animal has eaten him up.
Joseph must have been torn to pieces."

Jacob tore his clothes. He put on sackcloth.
Then he wept for his son for many days.

All Jacob's other sons and daughters came to comfort him.
But they weren't able to.

The traders sold Joseph to Potiphar, one of Pharaoh's officials.

Pharaoh's dreams

Pharaoh had a dream. In his dream, seven cows came up out of the river. They looked healthy and fat. After them, seven other cows came up out of the river. They looked ugly and skinny. The ugly, skinny cows ate up the seven cows that looked healthy and fat. Then Pharaoh woke up.

He fell asleep again and had a second dream.
In that dream, seven ears of corn were growing on one stem. They were healthy and good. After them, seven other ears of corn came up. They were thin and dried up by the east wind. The thin ears of corn swallowed up the seven healthy, full ears. Then Pharaoh woke up.

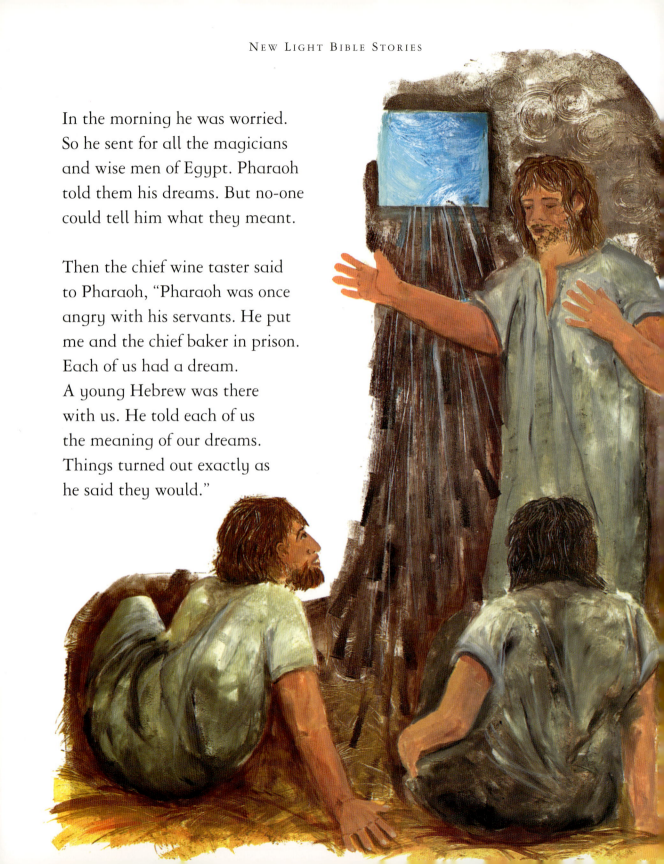

In the morning he was worried. So he sent for all the magicians and wise men of Egypt. Pharaoh told them his dreams. But no-one could tell him what they meant.

Then the chief wine taster said to Pharaoh, "Pharaoh was once angry with his servants. He put me and the chief baker in prison. Each of us had a dream. A young Hebrew was there with us. He told each of us the meaning of our dreams. Things turned out exactly as he said they would."

PHARAOH'S DREAMS

So Pharaoh sent for Joseph.

Pharaoh said to Joseph, "I've heard that when you hear a dream you can explain it."

"I can't do it," Joseph replied. "But God will give Pharaoh the answer he wants."

Then Pharaoh told Joseph what he had dreamed.

Joseph said to Pharaoh, "Both of Pharaoh's dreams have the same meaning. God has shown Pharaoh what he's about to do.

"Seven years with plenty of food are coming to the whole land of Egypt. But seven years when there won't be enough food will follow them.

"Pharaoh should appoint officials to be in charge of the land. He should give them authority to store up the corn. It will be needed when there isn't enough food in Egypt. Then the country won't be destroyed because it doesn't have enough food."

Then Pharaoh said to Joseph, "No-one is as wise and understanding as you are. You will be in charge of my palace. All my people must obey your orders."

Pharaoh took his ring off his finger. He put it on Joseph's finger. He dressed him in robes that were made out of fine linen.

He put a gold chain round his neck. Joseph was now second in command after Pharaoh.

During the seven years when there was plenty of food, Joseph stored up huge amounts of corn.

Then came the seven years when there wasn't enough food. Joseph opened the storerooms. He sold corn to the Egyptians. People from all the other countries also came to buy corn from Joseph.

Joseph and his brothers

Jacob found out that there was corn in Egypt. So he said to his sons, "I've heard there's corn in Egypt. Go down there. Buy some for us. Then we'll live and not die."

So ten of Joseph's brothers went down to Egypt to buy corn there.

As soon as Joseph saw his brothers he recognised them.
But they didn't recognise him.

He said to them, "You are spies!"

"No, sir," they answered. "We've come to buy food. We were 12 brothers. Our youngest brother, Benjamin, is now with our father. And one brother is gone."

Joseph said, "I still say you are spies! So I'm going to put you to the test. Send one of you back to get your brother. The rest of you will be kept in prison. Then we'll find out whether you are telling the truth."

They said to one another, "God is certainly punishing us because of our brother. He begged us to let him live. But we wouldn't listen."

They didn't realise that Joseph could understand what they were saying. He was using someone else to explain their words to him in the Egyptian language.

NEW LIGHT BIBLE STORIES

Joseph turned away from them and began to cry.
Then he turned round and spoke to them again.
He had Simeon taken and tied up right there in front of them.

Joseph gave orders to have their bags filled with corn.
He had each man's money put back into his sack.

They came to their father Jacob in the land of Canaan.
They told him everything that had happened to them.

Then they began emptying their sacks.
There in each man's sack was his bag of money!
When they saw the money-bags they were afraid.

JOSEPH AND HIS BROTHERS

After a while Jacob's family had eaten all of the corn the brothers had brought from Egypt.

So their father said to them, "Go back. Buy us a little more food."

Judah said, "Send our brother Benjamin along with us. I myself promise to keep him safe and bring him back to you."

Their father said, "If that's the way, it has to be, take some gifts and twice the amount of money with you."

So they hurried down to Egypt and went to Joseph.

The manager brought Simeon out to them and took them to Joseph's house.

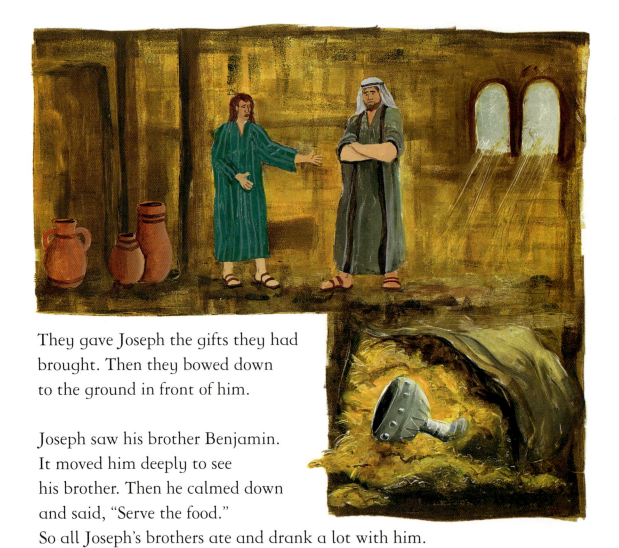

They gave Joseph the gifts they had brought. Then they bowed down to the ground in front of him.

Joseph saw his brother Benjamin. It moved him deeply to see his brother. Then he calmed down and said, "Serve the food."
So all Joseph's brothers ate and drank a lot with him.

Later, Joseph told the manager, "Put my silver cup in the youngest one's sack."

When morning came the men were sent on their way with the donkeys. Later Joseph sent the manager to catch them up and search their sacks. The cup was found in Benjamin's sack.

JOSEPH AND HIS BROTHERS

Joseph was still in the house when Judah and his brothers came in.

Joseph said, "The man who was found to have my cup will be my slave. The rest of you may go back to your father in peace."

But Judah said, "I promised my father I would keep the boy safe. Let me be your slave in place of the boy. Let the boy return with his brothers.
Don't let me see the pain and suffering that would come to my father."

Joseph couldn't control himself any more.

He said to his brothers, "I am your brother Joseph.
I'm the one you sold into Egypt. But don't be angry with yourselves.
It wasn't you who sent me here. It was God.
He made me ruler of the whole land of Egypt.

"Hurry back to my father. Bring him down to me. You will live
in the area of Goshen. There I will provide everything you need."

Then Joseph kissed all his brothers and cried over them.

After that his brothers talked with him.

Then they went up out of Egypt. They came to their father, Jacob,
in the land of Canaan. They told him, "Joseph is still alive!
In fact, he is ruler of the whole land of Egypt."

Moses and the burning bush

Jacob and his descendants were called Israelites. The Israelites lived in Egypt for a long time. But a new Pharaoh came to power in Egypt. He made the Israelites into slaves.

One of the Israelites was called Moses. He had run away from Egypt and was looking after the flock of his father-in-law Jethro in the desert.

One day the angel of the Lord appeared to him from inside a burning bush.

The Lord said, "I have seen my people suffer in Egypt. So now, go. I am sending you to Pharaoh. I want you to bring the Israelites out of Egypt."

But Moses spoke to God, "Who am I that I should bring the Israelites out of Egypt?"

God said, "I will be with you."

Moses said, "Please send someone else to do it."

MOSES AND THE BURNING BUSH

Then the Lord's anger burned against Moses. He said, "What about your brother Aaron? Tell him what to say. I will help both of you speak. I will teach you what to do."

So Moses and Aaron went to Pharaoh. They said,
"The Lord is the God of Israel. He says, 'Let my people go.
Then they will be able to hold a feast in my honour in the desert.'"

Pharaoh said, "Who is the Lord?
I won't let Israel go."

The plagues of Egypt

Aaron held out his stick in front
of Pharaoh and his officials.
He struck the water of
the River Nile. And all the
water turned into blood.

But the Egyptian magicians
did the same by their magic
tricks. So Pharaoh's heart
became stubborn.

Then Aaron reached out his hand over the
waters. And frogs came up and covered the land.

But the magicians did the same by their magic tricks.
And when Pharaoh saw that the frogs were dead,
his heart became stubborn.

Then Aaron struck the dust on the ground. And the dust all over the land of Egypt turned into gnats.

The magicians tried to produce gnats by their magic tricks. But they couldn't. Yet Pharaoh's heart was stubborn.

Then huge numbers of flies poured into Pharaoh's palace. All over Egypt, except in Goshen, the flies destroyed the land.

Pharaoh said, "I will let your people go to offer sacrifices. But you must not go very far."

Moses answered, "As soon as I leave you, I will pray to the Lord. Tomorrow the flies will leave you."

So the flies left Pharaoh, his officials and his people. But Pharaoh's heart became stubborn this time also.

The next day all the animals of the Egyptians died. But not one animal that belonged to the Israelites died. Yet Pharaoh's heart was still stubborn. He wouldn't let the people go.

Then Moses and Aaron took ashes from a furnace and stood in front of Pharaoh.
Moses tossed the ashes into the air and boils broke out on people and animals alike. The bodies of all the Egyptians were covered with boils.

But Pharaoh wouldn't listen to Moses and Aaron.

Then, all over Egypt, hail struck everything in the fields. It fell on people and animals alike. The only place hail didn't fall was in the area of Goshen. That's where the people of Israel were.

Pharaoh sent for Moses and Aaron. He said, "Pray to the Lord because we have had enough thunder and hail. I'll let you and your people go."

But when Pharaoh saw that the rain, hail and thunder had stopped, he wouldn't let the people go.

Then the Lord made an east wind blow across the land. By morning the wind had brought the locusts. They ate up everything that was growing in the fields.

Pharaoh quickly sent for Moses and Aaron. He said, "I have sinned against the Lord your God. Pray to the Lord your God to take this deadly plague away from me."

So Moses prayed to the Lord. The Lord changed the wind to a very strong west wind. The wind picked up the locusts. It blew them into the Red Sea.

But Pharaoh wouldn't let the people of Israel go.

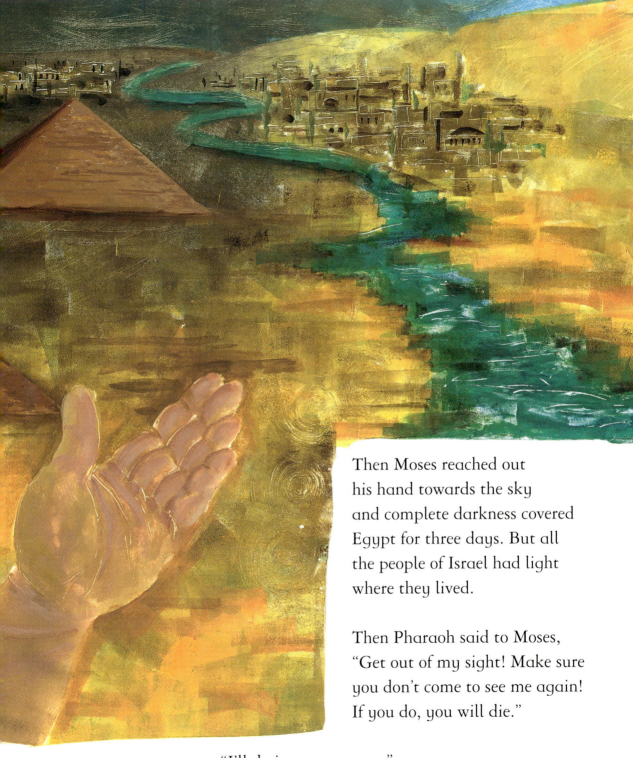

Then Moses reached out his hand towards the sky and complete darkness covered Egypt for three days. But all the people of Israel had light where they lived.

Then Pharaoh said to Moses, "Get out of my sight! Make sure you don't come to see me again! If you do, you will die."

"I'll do just as you say," Moses replied. "I will never come to see you again."

The Lord said to Moses, "I will bring one more plague on Pharaoh and on Egypt. After that he will let you and your people go."

Then Moses went to Pharaoh and said, "Every eldest son in Egypt will die. There will be loud crying all over Egypt. It will be worse than it's ever been before. And nothing like it will ever be heard again."

At midnight there was loud crying in Egypt because someone had died in every home.

The great escape

During the night Pharaoh sent for Moses and Aaron. He said, "Get out of here! Go. Worship the Lord. Take your flocks and herds. And also give me your blessing."

The Egyptians begged the people of Israel to hurry up and leave the country. So they marched out of Egypt like an army.

God led the Israelites towards the Red Sea through the desert. By day the Lord went ahead of them in a pillar of cloud. At night he led them with a pillar of fire.

The Egyptians went after the Israelites. They caught up with them as they camped by the sea.

The Israelites were terrified. But the Lord pushed the sea back with a strong east wind. The waters were divided and the people of Israel went through the sea on dry ground.

The Egyptians chased them into the sea. But the sea went back to its place and covered the army of Pharaoh.

The Israelites saw the great power the Lord showed against the Egyptians. So they had respect for him and put their trust in him and in his servant Moses.

David and Goliath

After many years in the desert, the
Israelites settled in Canaan
and were ruled over by judges
and then by kings.
Their first king was Saul.

One day Saul sent
messengers to a man
called Jesse. He said,
"Send me your son
David, the one who
looks after your sheep."

So David went to Saul and
began to serve him.

The Philistines were the enemies of the Israelites. A mighty hero named Goliath came out of the Philistine camp.

He stood and shouted to the soldiers of Israel, "Choose one of your men. If he's able to fight and kill me, we'll become your slaves. But if I win and kill him, you will become our slaves and serve us."

Every morning and evening for 40 days Goliath came forward.

Saul and the whole army of Israel were terrified.

David went backwards and forwards from Saul's camp to Bethlehem to look after his father's sheep.

Early one morning, he left his father's flock in the care of a shepherd and set out. He reached the camp just as the army was going out to its battle positions.

DAVID AND GOLIATH

Then he asked the men who were standing near him, "What will be done for the man who kills this Philistine? He dares the armies of the living God to fight him. Who does he think he is?"

Someone heard what David said and reported it to Saul. So Saul sent for him. David said to Saul, "I'll go out and fight. The Lord will save me from the hand of this Philistine."

Saul said to David, "Go. And may the Lord be with you."

David went down to a stream and chose five smooth stones.

NEW LIGHT BIBLE STORIES

Then he took his sling in his hand and approached Goliath.

He took out a stone and put it in his sling. He slung it at Goliath. The stone hit him on the forehead. He fell to the ground on his face.

Then David ran and stood over him. He took hold of Goliath's sword and cut off his head.

The Philistines saw that their hero was dead. So they ran away.

From that time on Saul kept David with him.
He didn't let him return to his father's home.

Daniel in the lions' den

At one time the Israelites were defeated in battle by the Babylonians. Among those who were taken captive to Babylon was a man called Daniel.

Darius, king of Babylon, appointed 120 royal rulers over his entire kingdom. He placed three leaders over them.

One of the leaders was Daniel. He did a better job than the other two leaders. So the king planned to put him in charge of the whole kingdom.

But the other two leaders and the royal rulers tried to find something wrong with the way Daniel ran the government. But they weren't able to. He could always be trusted.

So they went to the king and said, "We want to make a suggestion. King Darius, during the next 30 days don't let any of your people pray to any god or man except you. If they do, throw them into the lions' den. Give the order. Write it down. Then it can't be changed."

So King Darius put the order in writing.

Daniel found out that the king had signed the order. In spite of this, he did just as he had always done before. He went to his room three times a day to pray.

Some of the royal officials saw him praying. So they went to the king.

They said, "Daniel doesn't obey the order you put in writing. He still prays to his God three times a day."

When the king heard this, he was very upset. But he gave the order.

So Daniel was brought out and thrown into the lions' den.

The king returned to his palace. He didn't eat anything that night. And he couldn't sleep.

New Light Bible Stories

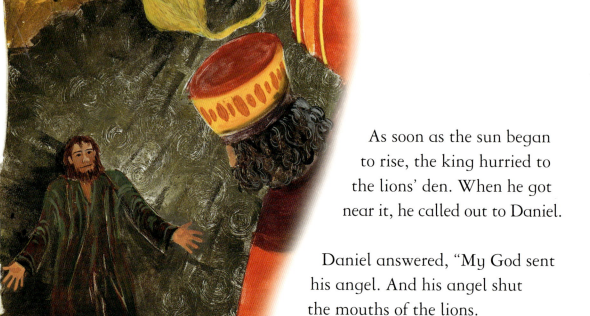

As soon as the sun began to rise, the king hurried to the lions' den. When he got near it, he called out to Daniel.

Daniel answered, "My God sent his angel. And his angel shut the mouths of the lions. They haven't hurt me at all. That's because I haven't done anything wrong in God's sight. I've never done anything wrong to you either, my king."

The king was filled with joy. He ordered his servants to lift Daniel out of the den.

Then the king gave another order. The men who had said bad things about Daniel were brought in. They were thrown into the lions' den. Before they hit the bottom of the den, the lions attacked them.

King Darius wrote: "I order people in every part of my kingdom to respect and honour Daniel's God. He is the living God. His rule will never end. He has saved Daniel from the power of the lions."

So Daniel had success while Darius was king.

Jonah and the storm

One day a message from the Lord came to a prophet called Jonah.

"Go to the great city of Nineveh. Preach against it. The sins of its people have come to my notice."

But Jonah ran away. He went down to the port of Joppa. Then he sailed for Tarshish.

But the Lord sent a strong wind over the sea. A fierce storm came up. All the sailors were afraid. But Jonah had gone below deck. There he lay down and fell into a deep sleep.

Jonah And The Storm

The sailors said to one another, "Let's cast lots to find out who is to blame for getting us into all this trouble." So they did. And Jonah was picked.

They found out that he was running away from the Lord. So they asked him, "What should we do to you to make the sea calm down?"

"Pick me up and throw me into the sea," he replied.

The men did their best to row back to land. But they couldn't. They prayed, "Lord, please don't let us die for taking this man's life."

Then they took Jonah and threw him overboard.
And the stormy sea became calm.

But the Lord sent a huge fish to swallow Jonah. And Jonah
was inside the fish for three days and three nights.

From inside the fish, Jonah prayed to the Lord.

The Lord gave the fish a command.
And it spat Jonah up on to dry land.

A message came to Jonah for a second time.

"Go to the great city of Nineveh."
Jonah obeyed the Lord.

He went to Nineveh and announced, "In 40 days Nineveh will be destroyed."

The people of Nineveh believed God's warning.

The news reached the king of Nineveh. He sent out a message to the people: "All of you must call out to God with all your hearts. Stop doing what is evil. God might take pity on us. He might turn away from his burning anger."

God saw what they did. They stopped doing what was evil. So he took pity on them. He didn't destroy them as he had said he would.

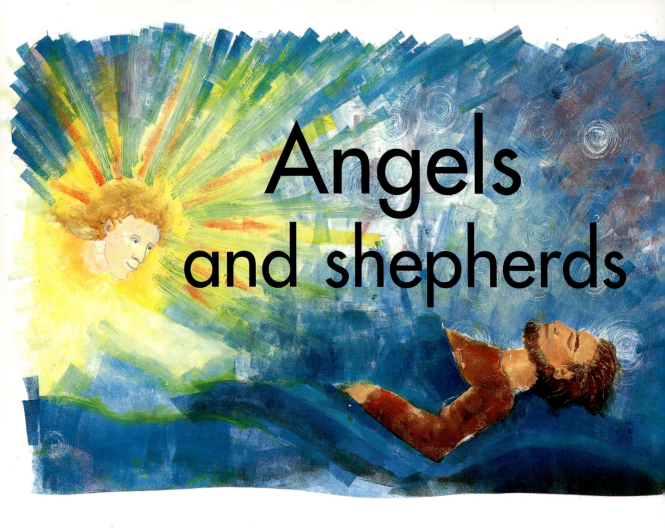

Angels and shepherds

Joseph was a descendant of Jacob. He and Mary had promised to get married.

But before they started to live together, Mary became pregnant by the power of the Holy Spirit. Joseph was a good man. So he planned to divorce her quietly.

But an angel of the Lord appeared to him in a dream and said, "Don't be afraid to take Mary home as your wife. The baby inside her is from the Holy Spirit. She is going to have a son. You must give him the name Jesus. This is because he will save his people from their sins."

ANGELS AND SHEPHERDS

Joseph took Mary home as his wife.

In those days Caesar Augustus made a law that everyone should go to their own towns to be registered. So Joseph went from Nazareth to Bethlehem with Mary.

While they were there, Mary gave birth to her first baby. She wrapped him in large strips of cloth. Then she placed him in a manger.

There was no room for them at the inn.

There were shepherds living out in the fields nearby.

An angel of the Lord appeared to them and said, "Do not be afraid. I bring you good news of great joy. Today in Bethlehem a Saviour has been born, Christ the Lord. You will find him wrapped in strips of cloth and lying in a manger."

Suddenly a large group of angels appeared, praising God.

Then the shepherds said, "Let's go to Bethlehem."

So they hurried off and found Mary and Joseph and the baby, Jesus.

Three wise men

The Shepherds told everyone what the angel had said about the child.
All who heard it were amazed.

Later, Wise Men from the east came to Jerusalem.
They asked, "Where is the child who has been born king of the Jews?
We saw his star and now we have come to worship him."

When Herod, king of Judea, heard about this, he was very upset.
He called together all the chief priests and teachers of the law
and asked them where the Christ was going to be born.

"In Bethlehem of Judea,"
they replied.

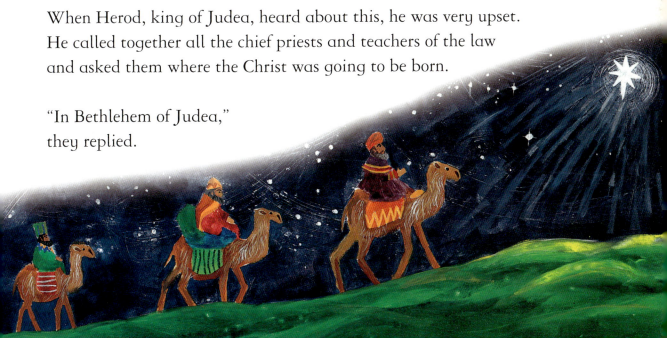

Then Herod sent the Wise Men to Bethlehem to search for the child. He said, "As soon as you find him, bring me a report. Then I can go and worship him, too."

The Wise Men went on their way. The star went ahead of them. It finally stopped over the place where the child was.

There they saw Jesus with his mother Mary. They bowed down and worshipped him. They gave him gold, incense and myrrh.

God warned them in a dream not to go back to Herod.
So they returned to their country on a different road.

Then Joseph had a dream. In it an angel of the Lord said to him,
"Escape to Egypt. Herod is going to search for the child.
He wants to kill him."

So Joseph left for Egypt with Jesus and his mother Mary.
They stayed there until King Herod died.

Loaves and fishes

Jesus grew up and left home. He went through all the towns and villages.
He preached the good news about the kingdom of God.
And he healed every disease and illness.

Then he called for his twelve disciples to come to him.
He gave them authority to drive out evil spirits and to
heal every disease and illness.

Here are the names of the twelve apostles: Simon Peter and Andrew; James
and John; Philip and Bartholomew; Thomas and Matthew;
James and Thaddaeus; Simon and Judas.

LOAVES AND FISHES

Jesus sent them out two by two.

Afterwards, they gathered
round him and told him
all they had done and taught.
But many people were coming
and going. So they did not even
have a chance to eat.

Then Jesus said to his apostles,
"Come with me by yourselves
to a quiet place. You need
some rest."

So they went away by
themselves in a boat
to a quiet place.
But many people ran from
all the towns and got there
ahead of them.

NEW LIGHT BIBLE STORIES

Jesus felt deep concern for them. They were like sheep without a shepherd. So he began teaching them many things.

His disciples said, "It's already very late. Send the people away. They can go and buy something to eat."

But Jesus answered, "You give them something to eat."

They said, "That would take eight months of a person's pay!"

"How many loaves do you have?" Jesus asked them.

They said, "Five loaves and two fish."

LOAVES AND FISHES

Then Jesus directed them to make all the people sit down in groups.

He looked up into heaven and gave thanks. He broke the loaves into pieces. Then he gave them to the disciples to set in front of the people. He also divided the two fish among them all.

All of them ate and were satisfied. The disciples picked up 12 baskets of broken pieces of bread and fish. The number of men who had eaten was 5,000.

Walking on water

Jesus made the disciples get into a boat.
He made them go on ahead of him to the other side
of the sea of Galilee. He sent the crowds away.

Then he went up on a mountainside by himself to pray.
When evening came, he was there alone.

The boat was already a long way from land. It was being pounded
by the waves because the wind was blowing against it.

Early in the morning, Jesus went out to the disciples. He walked on the lake. They saw him walking on the lake and were terrified.

"It's a ghost," they said and they cried out in fear.

Jesus called out to them. "Be brave! It is I. Don't be afraid."

"Lord, is it you?" Peter asked. "If it is, tell me to come to you on the water."

"Come," Jesus said.

So Peter got out of the boat. He walked on the water towards Jesus.

But when he saw the wind, he was afraid.
He began to sink. He cried out, "Lord! Save me!"

Jesus reached out his hand and caught him.

"Your faith is small," he said. "Why did you doubt me?"

When they climbed into the boat, the wind died down.

Then those in the boat worshipped Jesus. They said,
"You really are the Son of God!"

The good Samaritan

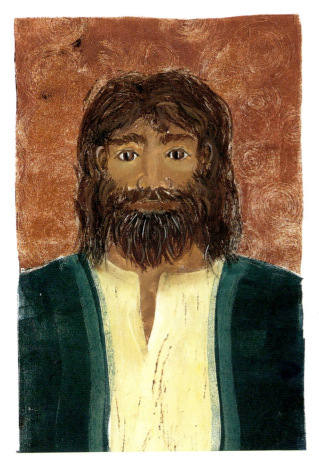

One day an authority on the law stood up to put Jesus to the test.

"Teacher," he asked, "what must I do to receive eternal life?"

"What is written in the Law?" Jesus replied.

He answered, "'Love the Lord your God with all your heart and with all your soul. Love him with all your strength and with all your mind.' And, 'Love your neighbour as you love yourself.'"

"You have answered correctly," Jesus replied. "Do this and you will live."

But the man wanted to make himself look good.
So he asked Jesus, "Who is my neighbour?"

Jesus replied, "A man was going down from Jerusalem
to Jericho. Robbers attacked him. They stripped off his clothes
and beat him. Then they went away leaving him almost dead.

"A priest happened to be going down that same road.
When he saw the man, he passed by on the other side.

"A Levite also came by. When he saw the man he
passed by on the other side too.

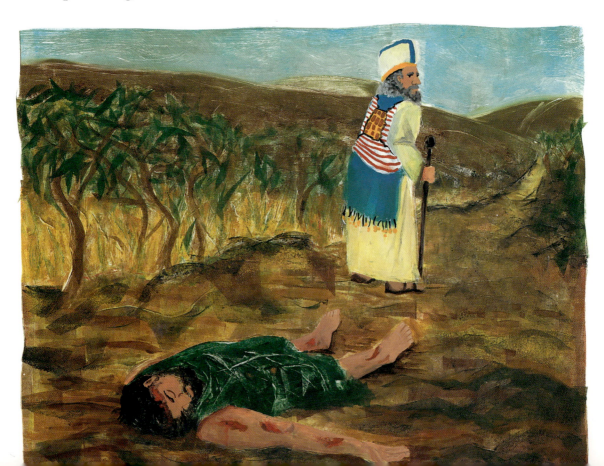

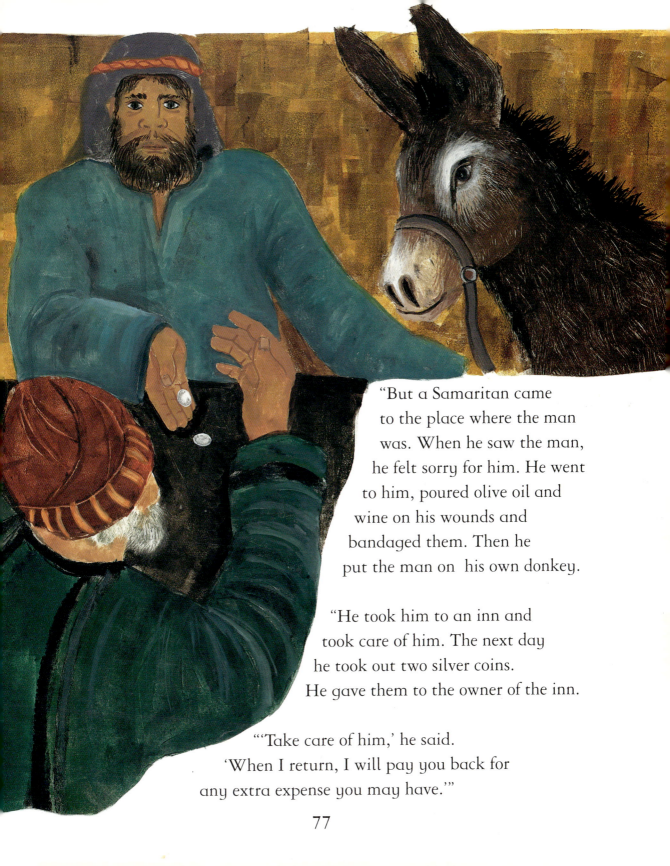

"But a Samaritan came to the place where the man was. When he saw the man, he felt sorry for him. He went to him, poured olive oil and wine on his wounds and bandaged them. Then he put the man on his own donkey.

"He took him to an inn and took care of him. The next day he took out two silver coins. He gave them to the owner of the inn.

"'Take care of him,' he said. 'When I return, I will pay you back for any extra expense you may have.'"

Then Jesus asked, "Which of the three do you think was a neighbour to the man who was attacked by robbers?"

The authority on the law replied. "The one who felt sorry for him."

Jesus told him, "Go and do as he did."

The loving father

The tax collectors and "sinners" were all gathered round to hear Jesus. But the Pharisees and the teachers of the law were whispering among themselves. They said, "This man welcomes sinners and eats with them."

Then Jesus told them this story.

There was a man who had two sons. The younger son spoke to his father. He said, "Father, give me my share of the family property."

So the father divided his property between his two sons.

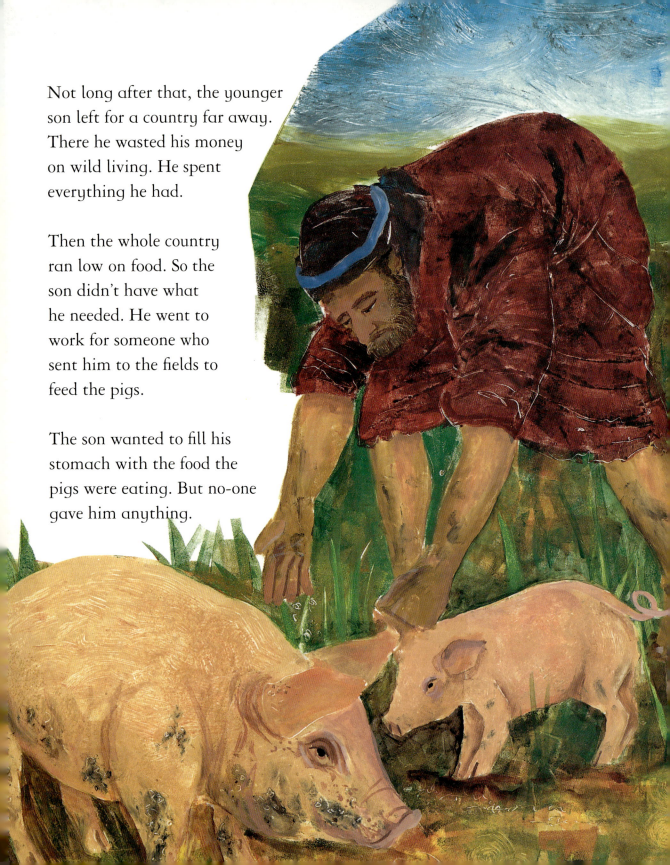

Not long after that, the younger son left for a country far away. There he wasted his money on wild living. He spent everything he had.

Then the whole country ran low on food. So the son didn't have what he needed. He went to work for someone who sent him to the fields to feed the pigs.

The son wanted to fill his stomach with the food the pigs were eating. But no-one gave him anything.

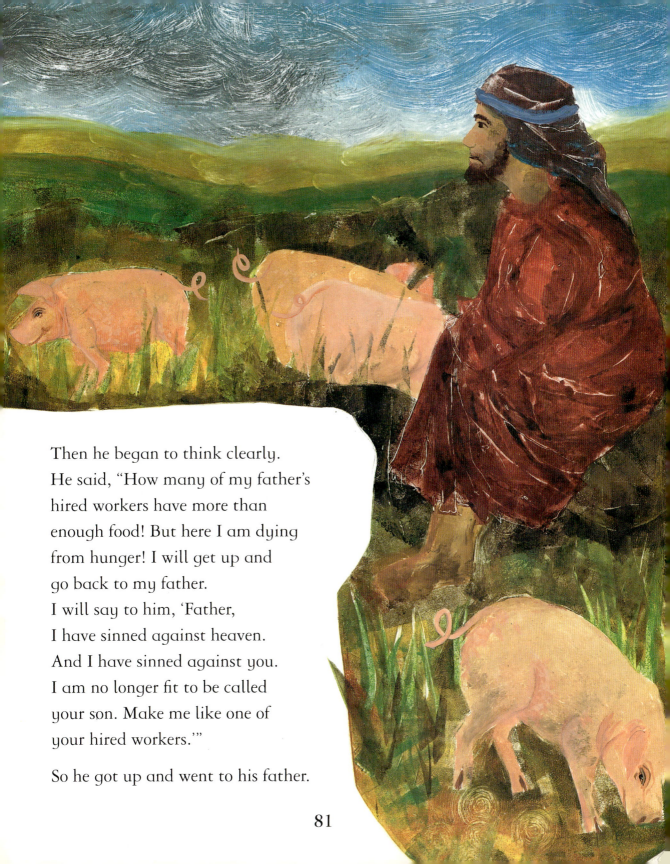

Then he began to think clearly. He said, "How many of my father's hired workers have more than enough food! But here I am dying from hunger! I will get up and go back to my father. I will say to him, 'Father, I have sinned against heaven. And I have sinned against you. I am no longer fit to be called your son. Make me like one of your hired workers.'"

So he got up and went to his father.

NEW LIGHT BIBLE STORIES

While the son was still a long way off, his father saw him. He was filled with tender love for his son. He ran to him. He threw his arms around him and kissed him.

The son said to him, "Father, I have sinned against heaven and against you. I am no longer fit to be called your son."

But the father said to his servants, "Quick! Bring the best robe and put it on him. Put a ring on his finger and sandals on his feet. Bring the fattest calf and kill it. Let's have a big dinner and celebrate. This son of mine was dead. And now he is alive again. He was lost. And now he is found."

The older son was in the field.

When he came near the house,
he heard music and dancing.
So he called one of the servants.
He asked him what was going on.

"Your brother has come home,"
the servant replied. "Your father
has killed the fattest calf."

The older brother became angry.
He refused to go in.
So his father went out
and begged him.

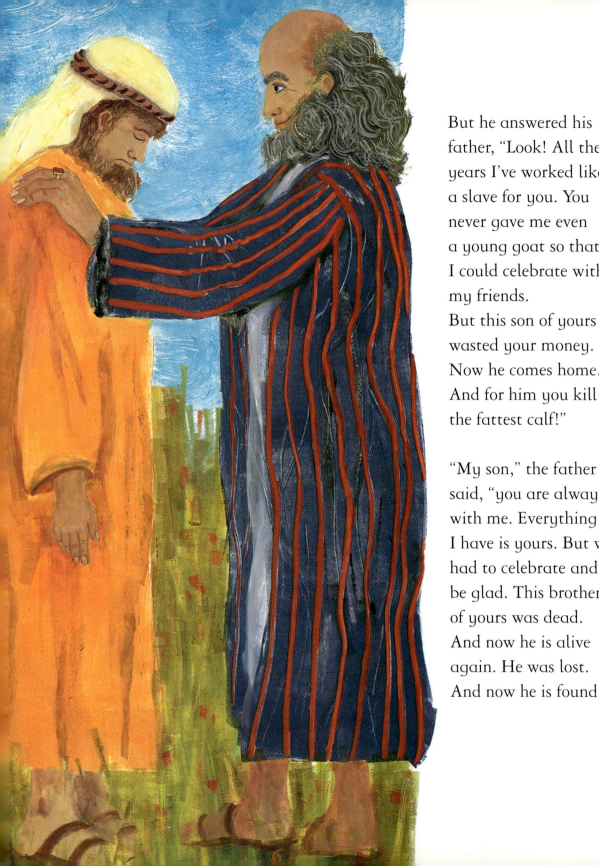

But he answered his father, "Look! All these years I've worked like a slave for you. You never gave me even a young goat so that I could celebrate with my friends.
But this son of yours wasted your money. Now he comes home. And for him you kill the fattest calf!"

"My son," the father said, "you are always with me. Everything I have is yours. But we had to celebrate and be glad. This brother of yours was dead. And now he is alive again. He was lost. And now he is found."

Zacchaeus
The tax collector

Jesus entered Jericho and was passing through. A man called Zacchaeus lived there. He was a chief tax collector and was very rich. He wanted to see who Jesus was. But he was a short man. He could not see Jesus because of the crowd. So he climbed a tree.

Jesus reached the spot where Zacchaeus was. He looked up and said, "Zacchaeus, come down at once. I must stay at your house today."

So Zacchaeus came down at once and welcomed him gladly.

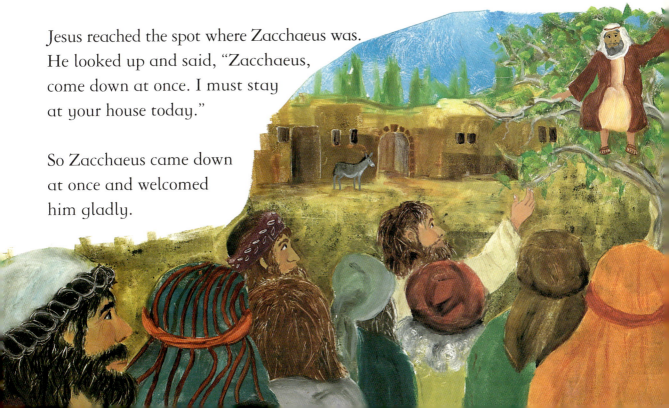

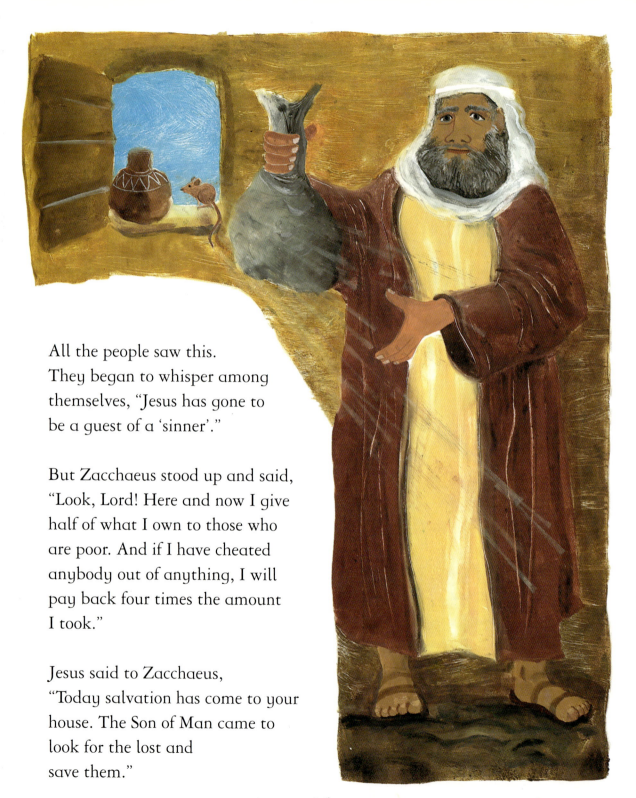

All the people saw this. They began to whisper among themselves, "Jesus has gone to be a guest of a 'sinner'."

But Zacchaeus stood up and said, "Look, Lord! Here and now I give half of what I own to those who are poor. And if I have cheated anybody out of anything, I will pay back four times the amount I took."

Jesus said to Zacchaeus, "Today salvation has come to your house. The Son of Man came to look for the lost and save them."

The road to Easter

Jesus and his disciples were on their way to Jerusalem.
Jesus took the twelve to one side.

He said, "The Son of Man will be handed over to the chief priests and the teachers of the law. They will sentence him to death They will flog him and kill him. Three days later he will rise from the dead!"

They came to the Mount of Olives. Jesus sent out two of his disciples.

He said to them, "Go to the village ahead of you. Just as you enter it you will find a donkey's colt tied there. No-one has ever ridden it. Untie it and bring it here."

So they brought the colt to Jesus. They threw their coats over it. Then he sat on it.

Many people spread their coats on the road. Others spread branches they had cut in the fields. They shouted, "Hosanna! Blessed is the one who comes in the name of the Lord!"

They were in Jerusalem on the first day of the Feast of Unleavened Bread.
So the disciples prepared the Passover meal.

While they were eating, Jesus took bread. He gave thanks and broke it.
He handed it to his disciples and said, "Take this and eat it. This is my body."

Then he took the cup. He gave thanks and handed it to them.
He said, "This is my blood of the new covenant.
It is poured out to forgive the sins of many."

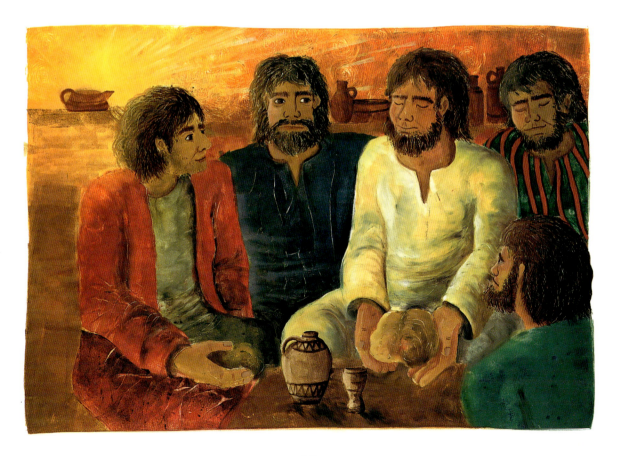

Afterwards Jesus went with his disciples to a place called Gethsemane.

Then he went a short distance from them. There he got down on his knees and prayed, Father, if you are willing, take this cup of suffering away from me. But do what you want, not what I want."

He went back to the disciples.

"Why are you sleeping?" he asked them.

While he was still speaking, a crowd came up. Judas was leading them. Then the men arrested Jesus and led him away.

Good Friday

The crowd took Jesus to the chief priests, the elders, and the teachers of the law. They all found him guilty and said he must die. Then they handed him over to Pilate.

The chief priests brought many charges against him. But Jesus did not reply.

"What shall I do with the one you call king of the Jews?" Pilate asked.

"Crucify him!" the crowd shouted.

"Why? What wrong has he done?" asked Pilate.

But they shouted even louder. Pilate wanted to satisfy the crowd. So he ordered that Jesus be flogged.

NEW LIGHT BIBLE STORIES

Then he handed him over
to be nailed to a cross.

Two other men were also led out
with Jesus to be killed. Both of
them had broken the law.

Jesus said, "Father, forgive them.
They don't know what they
are doing."

One of the criminals hanging
there made fun of Jesus.

But the other told him off.
Then he said, "Jesus, remember me
when you come into your
kingdom."

Jesus answered him, "Today you
will be with me in paradise."

The whole land was covered
with darkness until three o'clock.
Jesus called out, "Father, into your hands
I commit my very life."
After he said this, he took his last breath.

Joseph went to Pilate and asked for Jesus' body.
Then he put it in a tomb cut in the rock.

The empty tomb

The women who had come with Jesus from Galilee saw how Jesus' body was placed. Very early in the morning on the first day of the week, they went to the tomb. They found the stone rolled away from it.

When they entered the tomb, they did not find the body of the Lord Jesus. Suddenly two men in clothes as bright as lightning said to them, "Jesus is not here. He has risen!"

The women came back from the tomb. They told all these things to the others.

On the evening of that first day of the week, the disciples were together.

Jesus came in and stood among them. He said, "May peace be with you! The Father has sent me. So now I am sending you."

Thomas was not with the other disciples when Jesus came. He said, "I must see the nail marks in his hands and I must put my hand into his side. Only then will I believe."

A week later, when Thomas was with them, Jesus came in and stood among them.

He said to Thomas, "See my hands. Reach out your hand and put it in my side. Stop doubting and believe."

Thomas said to him, "My Lord and my God!"

NEW LIGHT BIBLE STORIES

After his death, Jesus appeared many times to his disciples. In many ways he proved that he was alive.

One day, he said to them, "You will receive power when the Holy Spirit comes on you. Then you will be my witnesses from one end of the earth to the other."

After Jesus said this, he was taken up to heaven.

Suddenly two men dressed in white clothing stood beside them.

They said, "Jesus has been taken away from you into heaven. But he will come back in the same way as you saw him go."